Application to Secede

This form is intended to assist small landmasses in the process of breaking away from their pre-existing political unions and establishing themselves as independent entities. It is not intended to be used to foment political unrest or guerilla warfare. Other forms are available for those express purposes.

Section 1: About you

1.1 Name

1.2 Present country of residence

1.4 What are your reasons for wanting to secede from your country of residence? (tick all that apply)

- ☐ Taxation
- ☐ Politics
- ☐ Culture
- ☐ Economics
- ☐ Sport
- ☐ Ethnicity
- ☐ Other

1.5 If the government of your present nation could change one thing to make you stay, what would it be?

Section 2: Your new nation

2.1 Name of new nation-state

2.2 Please give details of the area/landmass included within your new nation-state.
Use whatever description is most appropriate, eg street address, map co-ordinates, etc.

2.3 Broadly define your proposed system of government

- ☐ Republic
- ☐ Monarchy
- ☐ Dictatorship
- ☐ Parliamentary Democracy
- ☐ Religious Theocracy

2.4 Broadly define the political character of your new nation

- ☐ Fascist
- ☐ Liberal
- ☐ Communist
- ☐ Anarchist
- ☐ Social-Democrat

2.5 Provide a design for your new national flag
Use the space below. If you do not have coloured pens, you may use numbers to indicate shading.

2.6 The national anthem for my new nation will be...
Pick one only

☐ An existing song, namely

[ ] by [ ]

☐ A specially composed national anthem, entitled

[ ]

(If you wish to supply lyrics, please use additional sheets to do so.)

2.7 What currency will you be using in your new nation?
If you are planning to float your own currency, you will need to complete a "Licence to Print Money" form

[ ]

2.8 Does your new nation have a head of state?

☐ Yes
☐ No

2.9 Who is your head of state?

☐ Me
☐ Someone else, namely

[ ]

2.10 What is the head of state's official title? (King / Queen / President, etc.)

[ ]

2.11 Will you be applying for EU membership?

☐ Yes
☐ No

2.12 Will you be applying for a seat at the United Nations?

☐ Yes
☐ No

2.13 Please name 4 countries where you will be establishing embassies or consulates for your new nation.
One of these embassies or consulates must be in your former country of residence.

2.14 Will you be applying for loans/financial aid from any of the following institutions?

☐ International Monetary Fund
☐ World Bank
☐ Bank of England
☐ US Treasury
☐ European Union
☐ Bono

2.15 Please enter the amount you will be asking for in US$

$

Declaration of Independence

I, a duly appointed representative of the prospective nation of ______________________________, do hereby give notice that my people are no longer subjects of tyranny. From this day forth, we throw off the shackles of our oppressors and declare ourselves to be an independent nation.

Signature .... **Date**....................

Artistic Licence Application

An Artistic Licence allows the applicant to successfully create a tenuous relationship with reality, adjusting the world as he or she sees fit in order to conform with a specific aesthetic and social framework. In addition, a successful applicant shall bore people at parties and find any number of reasons not to get a proper job.

Section 1: Personal details

1.1 Name

1.2 Current occupation

1.3 Length of time in current occupation

	Years		Months

1.4 Satisfaction with current occupation

☐ Low ☐ Medium ☐ High

Section 2: Your artistic practice

2.1 What are the principle forms you work with?

- ☐ Painting
- ☐ Sculpture
- ☐ Installation
- ☐ Performance
- ☐ Film & Video
- ☐ Print
- ☐ New media
- ☐ Textiles
- ☐ Body mutilation/modification
- ☐ Intransigent, formless work that defies bourgeois classification

2.2 Have you ever exhibited your artwork before?

- ☐ Yes
- ☐ Exhibition is the enemy of creativity

2.3 Have you ever sold any artwork?

- ☐ Yes
- ☐ You call me a whore? I spit in your face

2.4 Have you studied for an art degree or diploma?

- ☐ Yes
- ☐ The only true artistic education one can receive is by living life with such an intensity that it burns everything it touches

2.5 Imagine you have made a piece of art called "Cascade". Describe the techniques used to create it in the space below. Your description should not include anything about the intent behind the work, only the physical processes used to make it. Metaphors and similes are not permitted. Nor is the word "juxtapose".

2.6 Now write the catalogue copy for the work "Cascade". In contrast to the previous question, your answer should be as obtuse and and self-indulgent as possible. Try to use words you don't understand.

Section 3: Your motivation

3.1 Do you want to be an artist?

- ☐ Yes
- ☐ It's complicated. In many ways, it's not so much that I want to become an artist, but rather that the current state of culture and society means that I have no other role to play. While I question the notion that some are predisposed towards artistic endeavour, it's a curious irony that I myself find no other form of labour that satisfies me.

3.2 Why do you want to become an artist?

3.3 Please indicate which artists you admire and why

- ☐ I do not admire anyone. They are all toads.

3.4 Sum up your artistic vision in one sentence

3.5 How true is this description?

- ☐ Very true
- ☐ Quite true
- ☐ Somewhat true
- ☐ Not at all true
- ☐ What is truth?

3.6 All waffle aside, what is your real motivation for becoming an artist?

- ☐ Getting laid
- ☐ Money
- ☐ Being famous
- ☐ Seems like fun
- ☐ I've seen some of the rubbish they put in galleries and figured I couldn't do any worse
- ☐ I just want someone to pay attention to me

Section 4: Draw a horse

Sign and date.....................................

Benefits Application

Friendship is great, but why limit yourself? Complete this application to add a sexual dimension to your previously platonic relationship. Applicants should be aware that submitting an application is no indication of its success and must agree to abide with the final decision.

Section 1: You

1.1 Forename

1.2 Surname

1.3 Your date of birth

DD | MM | YYYY

1.4 Your relationship status

- ☐ Single
- ☐ Sleeping around
- ☐ In a relationship
- ☐ Married
- ☐ Widowed
- ☐ Divorced

1.5 If in a relationship, who with?

1.6 Are they aware that you are making this application?

- ☐ Yes
- ☐ No

1.7 Date when you last had sex

We need this to determine your level of sexual desperation

DD | MM | YYYY ☐ Never

Section 2: Your friend

2.1 Friend's forename

2.2 Friend's surname (if known)

2.3 Friend's date of birth (or approximate age)

DD | MM | YYYY Age

2.4 Friend's relationship status

- ☐ Single
- ☐ Sleeping around
- ☐ In a relationship
- ☐ Married
- ☐ Widowed
- ☐ Divorced

2.5 If friend is in a relationship, who with?

Please provide as much detail as possible, but in case you don't have a name, then descriptions will suffice, e.g. 'The one with the dungarees'.

2.6 If friend is not in a relationship, when would you estimate they last had sex?

DD | MM | YYYY ☐ Never

2.7 Did they disclose this to you, or is this your own estimate?

- ☐ Disclosed
- ☐ Estimate
- ☐ Definite (I was involved or witnessed it)

Section 3: Your relationship

3.1 Categorise the friendship you have with this person

- ☐ Acquaintences
- ☐ Mates
- ☐ Chums
- ☐ Friends
- ☐ Partners in crime
- ☐ BFF

3.2 Indicate how long you have been friends

Please note that this is the length of your actual friendship, not just how long you have known each other

	hours		days		weeks		months		years

3.3 How did you meet?

- ☐ Work
- ☐ School
- ☐ Social occasion
- ☐ Team or club
- ☐ Church / place of worship
- ☐ Friend of a friend

3.4 When did you first realise that you were seeking benefits in this relationship?

DD	MM	YYYY

3.5 Do they have any idea that you are looking to add benefits to your friendship?

- ☐ Yes
- ☐ No
- ☐ Don't know

3.6 What sort of benefits are you looking for, exactly?

- ☐ Sex
- ☐ Companionship
- ☐ Relationship
- ☐ Life partner

3.7 On what basis are you looking for benefits?

- ☐ Temporary
- ☐ Permanent
- ☐ Unsure at this stage

3.8 Is it going to get weird?

- ☐ No
- ☐ Yes
- ☐ Definitely

3.9 Have you and this friend engaged in intimate behaviour prior to this application?

- ☐ No
- ☐ Almost, once, I think…
- ☐ Yes, we've kissed
- ☐ Yes, we fooled around a bit
- ☐ Yes, we've done the deed
- ☐ Yes, and then some

3.10 What happens if you one of you gets the feels?

- ☐ We talk about it like mature adults
- ☐ We end it right away
- ☐ We avoid talking about it until it becomes unbearable
- ☐ One of us finds another beneficiary, thus making this agreement null and void

3.11 Will you tell your friends / family?

- ☐ Yes
- ☐ No
- ☐ God, no

I am applying for benefits in good faith and all information provided is believed to be true at the time of submission. I promise to abide by the final decision and not get weird about it. Honest.

Signature .... **Date** ....

For respondent use only

- ☐ Accept
- ☐ Reject
- ☐ Pending further enquiry

Comments (optional)

Cloud Cuckoo Land – Application For Residency

If you're a free spirit, then come join us. We're all about free thinking, so please remember when filling out this form that there are no wrong answers.

Section 1: It's all about you, friend

1.1 What should we call you, compadre?

1.2 Where you staying right now? You got a place to crash?
- ☐ Not really, but that's OK. Living free's what it's all about, right?
- ☐ I'm kind of just hanging out, couch-surfing and staying on people's floors at the moment.
- ☐ Yeah, I'm staying with Sheila. You know Sheila, right? Such a good heart.
- ☐ I got, like, a place. It's here:

1.3 Permanent residency in Cloud Cuckoo Land requires forfeiture of home, job, family ties and all worldly possessions. Do you understand?
- ☐ Yeah, man, I get it
- ☐ No, I don't… what?
- ☐ Whatever you say. You're the boss.

Section 2: You might say that I'm a dreamer

2.1 Approximately how many hours a day do you spend daydreaming?
- ☐ Less than 1
- ☐ 1-2 hours
- ☐ 2-5 hours
- ☐ 6-12 hours
- ☐ More than 12 hours

2.2 Would you classify your grasp on reality as…
- ☐ Firm
- ☐ Light
- ☐ Tenuous
- ☐ Non-existent

2.3 Do you ever find yourself slipping into daydreams without consciously desiring to do so?
- ☐ Never – I'm always in control
- ☐ Sometimes – Daydreams sometimes sneak up on me
- ☐ Often – I don't know where I am half the time
- ☐ Always – I literally don't know what's real and what's not

2.4 How varied would you say your fantasies are?
- ☐ Very varied – I never have the same daydream twice
- ☐ Quite varied – I rarely imagine the same thing twice
- ☐ Somewhat varied – I sometimes like to revisit the same fantasies
- ☐ Not very varied – I usually go back to the same daydream
- ☐ Not at all varied – I imagine the same thing, over and over again

2.5 On your flights of fancy, which of these things would you say you daydream about *most*?

- ☐ Travel
- ☐ Exciting Adventures
- ☐ Fame
- ☐ Revenge
- ☐ Animals that talk/sing
- ☐ Time travel
- ☐ Rectifying past mistakes
- ☐ Getting married / Wedding day
- ☐ Home improvements
- ☐ Children
- ☐ Sex
- ☐ Flying

2.6 And which of these things would you say you daydream about *least*?

- ☐ Travel
- ☐ Exciting Adventures
- ☐ Fame
- ☐ Revenge
- ☐ Talking/singing animals
- ☐ Time travel
- ☐ Rectifying past mistakes
- ☐ Getting married / Wedding day
- ☐ Home improvements
- ☐ Children
- ☐ Sex
- ☐ Flying

2.7 Briefly describe your most interesting and/or exciting fantasy

2.8 Briefly describe your dullest and/or least exciting fantasy

2.9 If your application for permanent residency in Cloud Cuckoo Land is accepted, please specify your accommodation preferences

- ☐ I'd like to share my dreams with as many different people as possible (communal living space)
- ☐ I'd like to share my dreams with a few other people (shared living space)
- ☐ I'd prefer to keep my dreams to myself, thank you (private living space)

2.10 Have you ever had a dream so intense that when you woke up you weren't sure whether you had actually woken up or if you had just dreamt that you'd woken up and then that lead you to think that what if the dream you just had was actually part of a dream you had years ago that you still haven't woke up from and, like, how would you ever know if you were actually awake or dreaming and then you started to think "what's the difference?" and so you decided to live your life in that space between waking and dreaming?

- ☐ Yeah man. I totally get it. It's like, what is consciousness? We're only aware of it because our brains are thinking, but how crazy is it that our minds are aware of their own awareness? I think consciousness is like a box with mirrors on the inside, constantly reflecting themselves into infinity.
- ☐ No

I think the information I have given is true. I'm not sure… But anyway, thanks for taking the time to read my application.

Hope you're having a good day!

Signature .... **Date** ....

Declaration of Cold War

If you're in conflict with someone or something, but do not wish to engage in outright hostilities then please complete this form. A Declaration of Cold War allows you to engage in limited skirmishes without breaking the ongoing tension and thereby reaching an actual conclusion.

Section 1: Your details

1.1 Name

1.2 Have you ever declared war, cold or otherwise, before?

☐ Yes
☐ No

1.3 If YES, please give details here including who against, how long for and whether you felt you won

Against	Date	Outcome

Section 2: Enemy details

2.1 Name of principle enemy

2.2 Nature of principle enemy

☐ An individual
☐ A group of people
☐ An organisation, institution or business
☐ A government, nation or international political entity

2.3 Is your enemy aware of your intention to maintain a low-level confrontation over a long time frame?

☐ Yes
☐ No

2.4 Date when hostilities began

DD	MM	YYYY

2.5 Briefly describe the events and activities that led to your declaration of cold war

This statement will be used to determine the validity of your declaration. It is recommended that you include specific violations of policies, principles and norms that have led to this state of affairs. You may not use additional sheets.

Section 3: Strategic information

3.1 Main theatre of combat
This is where the bulk of your cold war will take place, but is not the exclusive site for hostilities. For example, 'in the break room', 'Sunday lunch' or ' on Facebook'.

3.2 Categorise your posture
- ☐ Aggressive
- ☐ Defensive
- ☐ Balanced

3.3 Give details of any forces allied to either you or your enemy
These allies may or may not know they are involved in the war effort.

Your allies	Enemy allies

3.4 While not wishing to reveal any tactical information that may compromise the waging of your war, we need to know the manner in which you intend to combat your opponent. Tick any and all methods at your disposal which you intend to use in your cold war campaign.
- ☐ Propaganda
- ☐ Limited physical skirmishes
- ☐ Sabotage
- ☐ Psychological manipulation
- ☐ Economic sanctions
- ☐ Cultural subversion
- ☐ Funding rivals and/or insurgents
- ☐ Hacking
- ☐ Misinformation
- ☐ Tampering with medicine and/or foodstuffs

Section 4: Ending hostilities

4.1 Estimated length of cold war

[ ] ☐ Days ☐ Weeks ☐ Months ☐ Years ☐ Forever

4.2 Your estimated probability of victory

[ ] %

4.3 Conditions necessary for you to voluntarily end hostilities and seek a peaceful accord with your enemy
These MUST be listed, no matter how unlikely or improbable they may seem

Section 5: Declaration

I, the undersigned, do hereby declare that a state of cold war exists between myself and the party or parties mentioned in Section 2.1 of this document. I agree to maintain a state of limited hostilities until the conditions of Section 4.3 are met, or until one or both of us has died or dissolved.

Signature .... **Date** ....

Disease of the Month Club

If you're tired of missing out on the hot new illnesses, sign up to the Disease of the Month Club. Every month, we'll send a new malady guaranteed to get you noticed by friends, family and doctors alike. All our diseases are transmitted by swab, syringe, sample jar or gas canister and are delivered in discreet plain packaging.

These are some of our most popular diseases and they're just 99p each!

D01 Alopecia – *Go smooth this season, with our hairloss special.*

D02 Bird Flu – *All the rage in 2004, this virus is still going strong.*

D03 Meningitis – *Inject a bit of drama into your life. Meningitis isn't just for kids, you know!*

D04 Bacterial gastroenteritis – *If you like it 'out both ends', this is the one for you.*

D05 Bebesiois – *A delightful malarial that's spread by ticks.*

D06 Pneumonia – *The old favourite, lovingly packaged for you.*

D07 Black piedra – *A fungal hair disease. Just as sexy as it sounds.*

D08 Botulism – *The disease behind Botox. It won't make you famous, but it's certainly something to talk about.*

D09 Brazilian hemorrhagic fever – *Samba and Sabia meet in this high infectious Latin American number.*

D10 Candidasis – *That's thrush to you and me. A popular choice with the ladies.*

D11 Chicken Pox – *A childhood favourite. If you haven't had it yet, now's the time!*

D12 Cholera – *The dirty water disease that just won't go away.*

D13 Colorado Tick Fever – *Let the bloodsucker work their magic in this hot import from the USA.*

D14 Common Cold – *Always handy to have in the cupboard, particularly if you don't feel like going to work!*

D15 Diptheria – *Get your bull-neck on with this oft-forgotten favourite.*

D16 Enterobiasis – *Have you taken the tape test?*

D17 Gonorrhoea – *Get yourself a reputation with this popular STD.*

D18 Hepatitis lucky dip – *A, B,C, D or E? You'll receive one of them at random with our mystery selection.*

D19 Keratitis – *Inflamed corneas are the name of the game with this ocular disease.*

D20 Legionnaire's Disease – *Serve your country with this patriotic infection.*

D21 Leprosy – *Try a new look this season.*

D22 Measles – *Another schoolyard classic. Red spots for everyone!*

D23 Mumps – *Life's swell when you've got the mumps. (Warning, may cause infertility.)*

D24 Nocardosis – *This difficult-to-diagnose disease has been called "the great imitator". See if your GP makes the grade!*

D25 Onchocerciasis – *Classic river blindness. Boaters beware!*

D26 Parrot Fever – *Who's a pretty boy then?*

D27 Pertussis – *Whoop! There it is…*

D28 Public lice – *Say hello to your new best friends.*

D29 Q Fever – *Little is known about this obligate pathogen. Be the first in your neighbourhood to come down with it.*

D30 Rabies – *A European favourite, this neuroinvasive virus will have you foaming at the mouth with excitement.*

D31 Ringworm – *The disease that circles the world*

D32 Rubella – *Ich bin ein German Measle.*

D33 SARS – *This respitory disease is due for a comeback. Start the revival, spread the word.*

D34 Salmonella – *Another classic stomach bug with all the hallmarks you can rely on.*

D35 Syphilis – *Al Capone's favourite is yours to keep.*

D36 Tetanus – *Lock your jaw and bolt your door, because tetanus is making a comeback.*

D37 Tuberculosis – *TB is a real wheeze, so share it with your friends.*

D38 Tularemia – *It could be the next great biological weapon, so get in early.*

D39 West Nile Virus – *With symptoms including coma, diarrhea and loss of appetite, this is perfect for all you calorie-counting slimmers out there.*

D40 Yellow Fever – *If you like vomiting blood, this is the one for you.*

D41 Zygomycosis – *A rare fungal condition, this is one for the collector.*

But wait... there's more!

Join now and you'll receive our exclusive historical set ***Plagues of the Middle Ages***, featuring five medieval illnesses that were thought to be eradicated by modern science.[1]

[1] *Modern immune systems may be resistant to medieval diseases. We take no responsibility for customer immunity to this or any other diseases.*

Order details

I would like the following diseases for only 99p each as my extra-special introductory rate!

D	D	D
D	D	D

Name

Billing Address

Date of birth

DD	MM	YYYY

These diseases are for

- ☐ Myself
- ☐ Someone else

Name	
Address	

☐ Tick here for gift wrapping (£5.99 extra)

Are you currently enjoying any diseases, illnesses or maladies?

- ☐ Yes
- ☐ No

If YES, what?

On average, how often do you usually get a new disease?

Every ☐ weeks ☐ months ☐ years

Where do you usually get your diseases from?

- ☐ Hospital
- ☐ Doctor's Surgery
- ☐ In town
- ☐ Public transport
- ☐ Friends and family

And how long, on average, would you say your diseases last for?

☐ weeks ☐ months ☐ years

☐ Yes, I want to sign up to the Disease of The Month Club! Please send me my selections in discreet packaging as soon as possible.

☐ I understand that I will be billed for my introductory disease by invoice in a separate mailing.

☐ I promise to fulfil my minimum obligation of six diseases over the subsequent twelve-month period (provided I don't die in the meantime).

Signature .... **Date** ....

Drug Mule Application

We at the Calliente Drug Cartel like to think of ourselves as a family and we hope that you'll become one of us very soon. Please remember that being an international drug mule isn't always as glamorous as it sounds. While there is a lot of foreign travel, there's more to the job than jet-setting – it also involves a lot of ingestion, interrogation and defecation.

Section 1: About You

1.1 Name

1.2 Country of residence

1.3 Date of birth

Section 2: Your Documentation

2.1 Do you own a passport?
- ☐ Yes
- ☐ No

2.2 Was it obtained legally?
- ☐ Yes
- ☐ No

2.3 Who does it belong to?
- ☐ Me
- ☐ A friend
- ☐ A relative
- ☐ Someone I stabbed in a hotel toilet
- ☐ I don't know. I just paid the money and didn't ask any questions.

Section 3: Experience

3.1 Have you ever smuggled drugs before?
- ☐ Yes
- ☐ No

(If NO, go to straight to Part 4)

3.2 If YES, on whose behalf?
- ☐ My own, for personal use
- ☐ My friends
- ☐ A nice looking man I met on holiday
- ☐ A major international crime syndicate *(give details)*

Name	
Organisation	

3.3 Did you get caught?
- ☐ Yes
- ☐ No

If YES, please provide details

Imprisoned in	
Time served	

Section 4: Your Capacity

4.1 What's the maximum number of filled condoms you think you could swallow?

☐ condoms

4.2 Would you be willing to undergo a minor surgical procedure to expand your drug-carrying capabilities?
- ☐ Yes
- ☐ No

4.3 Do you have any of the following health issues that may adversely affect your ability to smuggle drugs?
- ☐ Heart condition
- ☐ Spastic colon
- ☐ High blood pressure
- ☐ Diabetes
- ☐ Acid stomach
- ☐ Twitchy eye

4.4 Would you describe your bowel movements as...
- ☐ Regular
- ☐ Erratic
- ☐ Constipated
- ☐ Cataclysmic

Section 5: Travel Preferences

5.1 Where would you like to fly?
Please note that while we do try to accomodate the wishes of our mules, you will fly where tell you to fly.

FROM	TO
☐ Afghanistan	☐ Austria
☐ The Bahamas	☐ Belgium
☐ Bolivia	☐ Canada
☐ Brazil	☐ Czech Republic
☐ Burma	☐ Denmark
☐ Colombia	☐ Finland
☐ Costa Rica	☐ France
☐ Dominican Republic	☐ Germany
☐ Ecuador	☐ Greece
☐ Guatemala	☐ Ireland
☐ Haiti	☐ Italy
☐ India	☐ The Netherlands
☐ Jamaica	☐ Norway
☐ Laos	☐ Poland
☐ Mexico	☐ Portugal
☐ Nigeria	☐ Russia
☐ Pakistan	☐ Spain
☐ Panama	☐ Sweden
☐ Paraguay	☐ Switzerland
☐ Peru	☐ UK
☐ Venezuela	☐ USA
☐ Don't care	☐ Don't care

Section 6: Legal queries

6.1 How would you summarise your attitude to the police and customs agencies?
- ☐ They do a difficult job very well
- ☐ They cut corners in a way that makes me uneasy
- ☐ They are all pigs and their mothers are whores

6.2 If questioned about who you are working for, will you…?
- ☐ Tell them everything
- ☐ Drop hints and then say nothing until they're willing to cut you a deal
- ☐ Say nothing

6.3 Which of the following statements best describes your attitude to torture?
- ☐ I respond well to torture.
- ☐ I can hold out for a while, but eventually I'm going to crack.
- ☐ Torture me all you want – I ain't saying diddly squat.

6.4 Finally, why do you want to become a drug mule?
- ☐ Money
- ☐ Travel
- ☐ Excitement
- ☐ You are holding little Pepe

Yes, I want to become a drug mule! I submit my application in full knowledge of the fact that I may be arrested, imprisoned or killed in the process. I look forward to hearing from you.

Signature .... **Date** ....

Euphemistic Medical Form

Please complete this form in as little detail as possible, using as much vague and obfuscating language as possible. It will greatly frustrate your medical practitioner and support staff and should lead to increased waiting times for your fellow patients.

Section 1: Personal details

1.1 Patient name

1.2 Title
- ☐ Mr
- ☐ Mrs
- ☐ Miss
- ☐ What's it to you?

1.3 Age
- ☐ Please don't tell my parents
- ☐ Old enough to know better, right?
- ☐ Don't patronise me
- ☐ Oh, you

1.4 I am enquiring about this medical problem for
- ☐ Myself
- ☐ A friend
- ☐ No, really, it's for a friend

Section 2: Very personal details

2.1 Have you done any of the following in the past 24 hours?
- ☐ The business
- ☐ The stuff
- ☐ The thing
- ☐ The boopsie
- ☐ The whoopsie-do
- ☐ The knick-knack
- ☐ The Durham tremble
- ☐ The tic-tac-toe
- ☐ The oi-oi, saveloy
- ☐ The mmm
- ☐ The big G
- ☐ The uncha-uncha-uncha

Section 3: Medical History

3.1 Were you referred here by someone?
- ☐ Yes
- ☐ No

3.2 If YES, who advised you to seek medical care?
- ☐ Another doctor
- ☐ Local clinic
- ☐ Man on bus
- ☐ Aunty Sandra
- ☐ Hairdresser
- ☐ Barman

3.3 Have you ever received treatment or medical advice for THIS condition before?
- ☐ They gave me a pamphlet, I think
- ☐ I'm not supposed to eat cheese
- ☐ They did say *something*
- ☐ I've been putting Savlon on it
- ☐ Betty says it's just my age
- ☐ What do they know about it?

3.4 Have you ever recieved treatment for ANY OTHER condition at a hospital before?
- ☐ That thing with my feet
- ☐ They thought I had a whatchamacallit
- ☐ I took those big tablets
- ☐ When they thought I had the same thing as Janice but it turned out I didn't
- ☐ When I had to do all those tests
- ☐ Cousin Mark's 18th
- ☐ That swelling that wouldn't go away
- ☐ You know very well when

Section 4: Nature of problem

4.1 Where is the problem located?

- ☐ Up top
- ☐ Down below
- ☐ Round the back
- ☐ At the front
- ☐ Underneath
- ☐ All over
- ☐ The edges
- ☐ Right in the middle
- ☐ Just inside
- ☐ Down this side
- ☐ On the tip
- ☐ Just… *there*

4.2 What is the nature of the problem?

- ☐ It doesn't quite…
- ☐ It's just a bit…
- ☐ There's too much…
- ☐ There's not enough…
- ☐ Nothing seems…
- ☐ I get all…
- ☐ It's like…
- ☐ Sometimes it's…
- ☐ It's sort of…
- ☐ I just feel like I don't have any…
- ☐ There's a kind of…
- ☐ I'm just not…
- ☐ There are times when it's…
- ☐ I've noticed it doing a…
- ☐ I found something sort of…
- ☐ Sometimes it's normal and sometimes it's all…
- ☐ It's… it's…

4.3 ...what?

- ☐ …voom
- ☐ …rrrgh
- ☐ …burble burble
- ☐ …clicky click-click
- ☐ …beurgh
- ☐ …brrr
- ☐ …dooooo
- ☐ …ssssss
- ☐ …huhhuhhuh
- ☐ …bang
- ☐ …bing
- ☐ …bong
- ☐ …whoosh
- ☐ …duh duh *duhhh*
- ☐ …vvssshh

4.4 How long has it been like this?

- ☐ A while, I suppose
- ☐ Not too long
- ☐ Don't know, really

4.5 When does this problem usually occur?

- ☐ All the time
- ☐ Comes and goes
- ☐ When I *you know*
- ☐ When it's cold. Or hot.
- ☐ Constantly. Except now.
- ☐ During *the curse*
- ☐ During *The Chase*
- ☐ Difficult to say
- ☐ When I eat
- ☐ When I don't eat
- ☐ *When Saturday Comes*
- ☐ In the morning. Maybe mid morning? Afternoon, really. When it gets dark. Bedtime. At night. When I'm asleep.

4.6 Any secondary symptoms?

- ☐ Yes
- ☐ No

If YES, please draw lines to connect aspects of all secondary symptoms

Whatnots… ○	○ …in… ○	○ …my nee-naws
Danglers… ○	○ …on… ○	○ …my bits
Thingies… ○	○ …around… ○	○ …the precious
Whoosits… ○	○ …crawling out of… ○	○ …our mutual friend
Fumblies… ○	○ …gushing out… ○	○ …my foo-foo
Ta-tas… ○	○ …seeping from… ○	○ …my business
Grumbles… ○	○ …out… ○	○ …my flask

I do hereby certify that information I have provided is complete and accurate to the best of my knowledge, except for the obvious things which are really nobody's business.

Signature .... **Date** ....

Now cross out the above and sign again below, using the name given in **Section 1.1**

Signature .... **Date** ....

Licence to Print Money

In these difficult economic times, more and more people are choosing to create their own currency. It's an easy alternative to working and the benefits are numerous. This form allows you to inform the treasury of your intent to create your own currency and covers all the pertinent details, including conversion rates and note designs.

Section 1: Treasury details

1.1 Name of treasurer

1.2 Why are you looking to establish a new treasury and establish a new currency?

- ☐ Disillusionment with current economic system
- ☐ Political experimentation
- ☐ Personal financial ruin

1.3 Please indicate which of the following financial institutions you have been responsible for

- ☐ National bank
- ☐ Commercial bank
- ☐ Investment fund
- ☐ Company accounts
- ☐ Club or society
- ☐ Personal finances
- ☐ Natwest Junior Saver account

Section 2: Currency details

2.1 Full name of new currency:

2.2 Three letter acronym
(For example, USD represents the US Dollar)

2.3 Currency symbol
(e.g. $, £, €)

2.4 Initial exchange rate for your new currency

	US Dollar	Euro	UK Pound
1 unit of your currency =			

2.5 How will you be printing your currency?

- ☐ Office photocopier
- ☐ Newsagent photocopier
- ☐ Home PC
- ☐ Each note will be hand-drawn

2.6 Please provide details of your anti-counterfeiting measures

2.7 Will your currency be linked to the trading price of another commodity?

- ☐ Yes
- ☐ No

2.8 If YES, what?

Section 3: Currency design

3.1 Please provide a design for the BACK of your notes, which will be used for ALL DENOMINATIONS

3.2 Please provide the face value and design for the FRONT of your LOW denomination note

Value

3.3 Please provide the face value and design for the FRONT of your MEDIUM denomination note

Value

3.4 Please provide the face value and design for the FRONT of your HIGH denomination note

Value

I declare that these are my own designs and that the proposed currency is not intended to pass for or supplant any other currencies that may already be in place. I affirm my status as a treasurer in good standing and reject any notion that I am a forger, counterfeiter or fraudster.

Signature .... **Date** ....

Life Exchange Application

If you have found your life to be unsatisfactory and has not lived up to your expectations, you may be entitled to return it and claim an alternative life of higher value.

Section 1: Your current life

1.1 Name

☐

1.2 Age

☐

1.3 Occupation

☐

1.4 Relationship status

- ☐ Single
- ☐ Long-term relationship
- ☐ Civil partnership
- ☐ Married
- ☐ Divorced
- ☐ Widowed

1.5 Number of children

☐

1.6 Tick ONE main problem you have had with your life

- ☐ Finances
- ☐ Emotional wellbeing
- ☐ Career
- ☐ Happiness
- ☐ Love life
- ☐ Loneliness
- ☐ Instability
- ☐ Physical Health
- ☐ Mental health
- ☐ Substance abuse
- ☐ Friendship
- ☐ Betrayal

1.7 Please state your greatest achievement, no matter how small it may seem to other people

☐

1.8 Please state your biggest regret

☐

1.9 What do you attribute your misfortune to?

- ☐ Bad luck
- ☐ Gypsy curse
- ☐ Conspiracy
- ☐ God hates me
- ☐ Other people
- ☐ Own laziness

1.10 How much of a role do you feel you have played in the dissatisfactory nature of your life?

- ☐ It's all my fault
- ☐ Some of it's down to me
- ☐ I've tried my best
- ☐ It's not my fault

1.11 Do you feel you've taken advantage of all the opportunities presented to you over the years?

- ☐ I've let some of them slip through my fingers
- ☐ I've done what I could
- ☐ I've pissed them all up the wall
- ☐ What opportunities?

Section 2: Your new life

2.1 Is there someone you wish you could swap lives with?

☐ Yes, namely ☐ No

2.2 If YES, why this person in particular?

☐ I want what they have ☐ They seem to have it sorted ☐ I want them to suffer like I have

2.3 Preferred career

2.4 Preferred relationship status

☐ Single ☐ Civil partnership ☐ Divorced
☐ Long-term relationship ☐ Married ☐ Widowed

If you know who you would prefer to be in a relationship with, name them here

2.5 Preferred number of children

2.7 Preferred place to live

2.8 Preferred method of transportation

2.9 Number one ambition to fulfil

2.10 Briefly make your case for exchanging your current life for your preferred one.

Section 3: In case of partial exchange

Exchanges are not always possible. Use this section to indicate which aspects you may use to improve your current life.

3.1 If there was one thing you could have MORE of in your current life, what would it be?

☐ Time ☐ Work ☐ Fun
☐ Money ☐ Family ☐ Health
☐ Sex ☐ Travel ☐ Responsibility
☐ Opportunity ☐ Education ☐ Luck

3.2 If there was one thing you could have LESS of in your current life, what would it be?

☐ Time ☐ Work ☐ Fun
☐ Money ☐ Family ☐ Health
☐ Sex ☐ Travel ☐ Responsibility
☐ Opportunity ☐ Education ☐ Luck

I hereby give notice of my intent to exchange my life and all it's trappings for another of equal or greater value as determined by an independent assessor. I understand that the exchange is permanent and non-refundable.

Signature .... **Date** ....

Multiple Personality Registration

Begin with your primary personality and work from there.
You may make additional copies of this form if you do not have enough space for all of you.

Name

Age

Gender
☐ Male ☐ Female ☐ Other

Species
☐ Human ☐ Alien ☐ Demon
☐ Animal ☐ Robot ☐ Angel

Occupation

Physical attributes of this personality
(e.g. hats, eyepatches, limps, etc.)

Broadly speaking, this personality is...
☐ Angry ☐ Neurotic
☐ Brave ☐ Obsessive
☐ Cruel ☐ Paranoid
☐ Decadent ☐ Quiet
☐ Egotistical ☐ Romantic
☐ Frail ☐ Selfish
☐ Generous ☐ Terrifying
☐ Happy ☐ Ugly
☐ Intellectual ☐ Vicious
☐ Joyful ☐ Weak
☐ Kind ☐ X-rated
☐ Lusty ☐ Youthful
☐ Manic ☐ Zany

Is this personality aware of the others?
☐ Yes ☐ No

If YES, how well do they get on with them?
☐ Well ☐ OK ☐ Badly

Signature ....

Name

Age

Gender
☐ Male ☐ Female ☐ Other

Species
☐ Human ☐ Alien ☐ Demon
☐ Animal ☐ Robot ☐ Angel

Occupation

Physical attributes of this personality
(e.g. hats, eyepatches, limps, etc.)

Broadly speaking, this personality is...
☐ Angry ☐ Neurotic
☐ Brave ☐ Obsessive
☐ Cruel ☐ Paranoid
☐ Decadent ☐ Quiet
☐ Egotistical ☐ Romantic
☐ Frail ☐ Selfish
☐ Generous ☐ Terrifying
☐ Happy ☐ Ugly
☐ Intellectual ☐ Vicious
☐ Joyful ☐ Weak
☐ Kind ☐ X-rated
☐ Lusty ☐ Youthful
☐ Manic ☐ Zany

Is this personality aware of the others?
☐ Yes ☐ No

If YES, how well do they get on with them?
☐ Well ☐ OK ☐ Badly

Signature ....

Name

Age

Gender

☐ Male ☐ Female ☐ Other

Species

☐ Human ☐ Alien ☐ Demon
☐ Animal ☐ Robot ☐ Angel

Occupation

Physical attributes of this personality
(e.g. hats, eyepatches, limps, etc.)

Broadly speaking, this personality is…

☐ Angry	☐ Neurotic
☐ Brave	☐ Obsessive
☐ Cruel	☐ Paranoid
☐ Decadent	☐ Quiet
☐ Egotistical	☐ Romantic
☐ Frail	☐ Selfish
☐ Generous	☐ Terrifying
☐ Happy	☐ Ugly
☐ Intellectual	☐ Vicious
☐ Joyful	☐ Weak
☐ Kind	☐ X-rated
☐ Lusty	☐ Youthful
☐ Manic	☐ Zany

Is this personality aware of the others?

☐ Yes ☐ No

If YES, how well do they get on with them?

☐ Well ☐ OK ☐ Badly

Signature ....

Name

Age

Gender

☐ Male ☐ Female ☐ Other

Species

☐ Human ☐ Alien ☐ Demon
☐ Animal ☐ Robot ☐ Angel

Occupation

Physical attributes of this personality
(e.g. hats, eyepatches, limps, etc.)

Broadly speaking, this personality is…

☐ Angry	☐ Neurotic
☐ Brave	☐ Obsessive
☐ Cruel	☐ Paranoid
☐ Decadent	☐ Quiet
☐ Egotistical	☐ Romantic
☐ Frail	☐ Selfish
☐ Generous	☐ Terrifying
☐ Happy	☐ Ugly
☐ Intellectual	☐ Vicious
☐ Joyful	☐ Weak
☐ Kind	☐ X-rated
☐ Lusty	☐ Youthful
☐ Manic	☐ Zany

Is this personality aware of the others?

☐ Yes ☐ No

If YES, how well do they get on with them?

☐ Well ☐ OK ☐ Badly

Signature ....

☐ Tick here if this is an additional photcopied sheet.
All sheets must be securely fastened together.

Sheet number		of	

New Airline Registration

If you have grown tired of lost luggage, plastic meals and tray tables that won't stay up, complete this form and you could be the one to inflict these miseries on others, rather than just sitting there and taking it like a chump.

Section 1: Airline details

1.1 Name of airline

1.2 Base of operations (country/city/airport)

1.3 Scope of operations

- ☐ International
- ☐ Domestic

1.4 What kind of flights will you be flying?

- ☐ Passenger
- ☐ Freight
- ☐ Both

1.5 Please give the estimated number of flights you will be running in an average week

1.6 Destinations your airline will fly to

Section 2: Your Fleet

2.1 Do you currently own any aircraft?

- ☐ Yes
- ☐ No

2.2 If YES, please give details here, including manufacturer, model and age of all aircraft you intend to use in your commercial activities

Manufacturer	Model	Age	Quantity

2.3 If NO, how do you intend to meet your schedules?

- ☐ Using other carriers' aircraft
- ☐ Stealing other carriers' aircraft
- ☐ Blindfolding passengers and making "nnnnrrrrowww" sounds while shaking their chairs
- ☐ We're just hoping that nobody will notice

Section 3: Branding And Livery

3.1 Please draw the logo of your airline

3.2 Airline slogan/motto

3.3 Please indicate the areas in which you feel your airline will be STRONGEST

- ☐ Customer service
- ☐ Cheap Fares
- ☐ Luxury service
- ☐ Legroom / passenger space
- ☐ Quality of meals
- ☐ Attractive cabin staff
- ☐ Variety of destinations
- ☐ Unusual destinations
- ☐ Safety

3.4 Please indicate the areas in which you feel your airline will be WEAKEST

- ☐ Customer service
- ☐ Cheap Fares
- ☐ Luxury service
- ☐ Legroom / passenger space
- ☐ Quality of meals
- ☐ Attractive cabin staff
- ☐ Variety of destinations
- ☐ Unusual destinations
- ☐ Safety

Section 4: Environmental impact

4.1 Please use the space provided to illustrate what steps you will be taking to offset the massive environmental damage done by long-haul air travel. Be as detailed as possible.

Section 5: Crew, safety and security

5.1 How many employees do you plan to employ?

	Pilots
	Cabin Crew
	Ground crew
	Administrative staff

5.2 Where do you intend to hire most of your employees from?

- ☐ Private sector (other airlines, aviation industry, etc.)
- ☐ Public sector (armed forces)
- ☐ Online flight simulator community
- ☐ Don't care

5.3 Increased security has changed the nature of air travel in the past few years. Please indicate what measures you have taken to ensure the safety of your passengers and employees

- ☐ Heightened security at check-in
- ☐ Increased baggage scanning and searching
- ☐ Bomb detection systems on aircraft
- ☐ Full cavity searches for all passengers
- ☐ Full cavity searches for attractive passengers
- ☐ Banning passengers with funny sounding names
- ☐ Banning passengers
- ☐ Alsatian cabin crew
- ☐ Nanobiotic inflight meals

I assert that the information I have given is complete and accurate to the best of my knowledge. In submitting this application, I hereby agree to comply with all international, domestic and local air transport regulations.
Most of them, anyway.

Signature .... **Date** ....

Nuisance Neighbour Form

Housing by-laws require a certain amount of troublesome householders per area. Complete this application to become a Nuisance Neighbour and enjoy the privileges that come with being an officially-mandated pest.

Section 1: About You

1.1 Name

1.2 Current address

1.3 Are you looking to stay here or relocate?

☐ Stay
☐ Relocate
☐ No preference

1.4 Current living arrangement

☐ Living alone
☐ Living with partner / spouse
☐ Living with housemates
☐ Living with family

1.5 Type of residence

☐ Detached house
☐ Semi-detached house
☐ Terraced house
☐ Bungalow
☐ Converted flat (part of a house)
☐ Purpose-built flat (part of a block)
☐ Caravan
☐ Shed

Section 2: Your habits

2.1 Which of the following do you enjoy on a constant, regular or occasional basis?

	Constant	Regular	Occasional	Never
Playing music (records, CDs)	☐	☐	☐	☐
Playing music (instrument)	☐	☐	☐	☐
Bonfires / other burnings	☐	☐	☐	☐
Arguing with spouse / family	☐	☐	☐	☐
DIY (drilling, hammering, etc)	☐	☐	☐	☐
Moving furniture	☐	☐	☐	☐
Collecting rubbish	☐	☐	☐	☐
Walking around in heavy boots	☐	☐	☐	☐
Karaoke	☐	☐	☐	☐
Nudism	☐	☐	☐	☐
Noisy sexual intercourse	☐	☐	☐	☐
Breaking and smashing	☐	☐	☐	☐
Taxidermy	☐	☐	☐	☐

2.2 Please give the maximum decibel level of your hi-fi/stereo

	Db

If your system is not of sufficient power, you may be eligible for an upgrade grant.

2.3 Do you leave your television on at night?

- ☐ Yes
- ☐ No

2.4 Do you have a drink and/or drug problem?

- ☐ Yes
- ☐ No

2.5 If YES, please tick the box that best describes you whilst intoxicated

- ☐ Violent
- ☐ Exuberant
- ☐ Paranoid
- ☐ Mournful

2.6 Please tick the box that best describes your current employment status

- ☐ Unemployed
- ☐ Drug dealer
- ☐ Sex worker
- ☐ Amateur DJ

2.7 How often are you at home?

- ☐ Constantly
- ☐ Never
- ☐ All day
- ☐ All night
- ☐ When you least expect it

2.8 How many times a week do you estimate the police will have to be called to your home?

	times a week

2.9 Do you have children?

- ☐ Yes, _______ children
- ☐ No

2.10 Do you have pets?

- ☐ Yes
- ☐ No

2.11 If YES, please provide details, including numbers, breeds and levels of domestication

	Number	Breed / type	Obedient	Excitable	Vicious	Feral
Cats			☐	☐	☐	☐
Dogs			☐	☐	☐	☐
Rats			☐	☐	☐	☐
Mice			☐	☐	☐	☐
Gerbils			☐	☐	☐	☐
Frogs			☐	☐	☐	☐
Snakes			☐	☐	☐	☐
Lizards			☐	☐	☐	☐
Fish			☐	☐	☐	☐

2.12 Please tick any items that you currently have in or around your house

- ☐ Disassembled car / motorbike
- ☐ Compost heap
- ☐ Pile of used nappies
- ☐ Soiled mattress
- ☐ Cockfighting pen
- ☐ Stolen goods
- ☐ Cadaver(s)

2.13 How do you intend to communicate with your neighbours?

- ☐ Insane, misspelled letters
- ☐ Late night phone calls
- ☐ Shouting through the walls/floor/ceiling
- ☐ Cut up ransom notes
- ☐ Banging and/or tapping
- ☐ Through solicitors only

I swear that the information I have given here may or may not be true, but if anyone calls me a liar or so much as looks at me funny, I'll put a flaming bag of dog poo through their letterbox.

Signature .... **Date** ....

Outrageous Claim Form

Everyone stretches the truth now and then, but there are times when each of us makes a statement which far exceeds the bounds of reasonable credibility. If you have made an Outrageous Claim, please complete this form in full in order to recieve proper credit and compensation for your remarkable whopper.

Section 1: Your details

It is vital that you provide accurate details in this section, even if your intended claim relates to any aspect of this information. False information may result in your claim being delayed or rejected and egregious falsehoods may require legal investigation.

1.1 Name

1.2 Date of birth

DD	MM	YYYY

1.3 Current occupation

Section 2: Type of claim

2.1 Please tick the box that best describes the type of claim you wish to make

- ☐ Claim to have been present somewhere
- ☐ Claim to know someone
- ☐ Claim to hold a world record
- ☐ Claim to have witnessed an event
- ☐ Claim to have played a sport or game at a high level
- ☐ Claim to have won something
- ☐ Claim to have performed a heroic deed
- ☐ Claim to have invented something
- ☐ Claim to have been the original author of a song / book / joke
- ☐ Claim to have beaten up someone
- ☐ Claim to have been beaten up by someone
- ☐ Claim to have held a position for which you are unqualified
- ☐ Claim to have special powers
- ☐ Claim to hold an academic qualifications
- ☐ Claim to be related to someone
- ☐ Claim to have never seen someone before in your life
- ☐ Claim to have had sex with someone
- ☐ Claim to have played with a musician or sports personality and shown them how it was done
- ☐ Claim to have seen a rare or mythical creature or phenomenon
- ☐ Other

2.2 BRIEFLY outline the specific claim you wish to make

2.3 How close is this claim to the truth?

- ☐ Exaggeration – Something like this happened, and I'm just stretching it a bit
- ☐ Hyperbole – I've taken a minor incident and blown it way out of proportion
- ☐ Misunderstanding – I don't know what I'm talking about
- ☐ Utter twaddle – I'm talking complete rubbish and I just don't care

2.4 And how believable to do you think this claim is?

- ☐ It's a stretch
- ☐ I mean, theoretically it's possible
- ☐ No way, José

2.5 Where are you planning to make this claim?

- ☐ In the pub
- ☐ At work
- ☐ In a job interview
- ☐ At a family gathering
- ☐ On the pull
- ☐ To literally anyone who will listen

2.6 How often do you intend to repeat this claim?

- ☐ Once only
- ☐ Now and then
- ☐ Regularly
- ☐ Repeatedly
- ☐ Constantly

2.7 Do you have anyone willing to back up your claim, regardless of their own knowledge or any sense of logic?

- ☐ Yes
- ☐ No

If YES, please give their name and contact details. We may need to find out what they're getting from it

Name	
Address	

2.8 If challenged to back up your claim, what will you say?

- ☐ "Of course, we don't talk anymore, so less said about it the better."
- ☐ "No, I lost all that stuff in the move. Pity, really…"
- ☐ "I've got the photos round at my mum's. I'll pick them up next time I'm round there."
- ☐ "You think I wasn't born then? You flatter me, pal!"
- ☐ "You can't prove anything."
- ☐ "Yeah? Well what have you ever done?"

2.9 Please indicate if you would like any documentary evidence to back up your outrageous claim. These items are made by experts and can help any claim appear convincing, no matter how audacious.

Please note that fake evidence may incur additional charges

- ☐ Altered photographs
- ☐ Fake letter
- ☐ Bogus certificates
- ☐ Phony newspaper

I understand that the claim I am making is totally unjustifiable and without foundation. Should I be caught out in my lie, I take the consequences as my own and will not blame anyone else for my inability to a) keep my gob shut and b) maintain any distinction between fantasy and reality.

Signature .... Date ....

Permission to Quit the Gym (Like a Bitch)

So, you're a quitter. That's your choice. Just fill out the form so we can learn more about your reasons for wussing out.

Section 1: Your Details

1.1 Name

1.2 Length of gym membership

☐ days ☐ weeks ☐ months ☐ years

1.3 How much can you bench?

1.4 How fast can you run 10k?

Section 2: Leaving the gym

2.1 Do you want to leave the gym?

☐ Yes, I want to leave the gym. ***Go to the next question***

☐ No, I've changed my mind and I'm sorry for wasting your time. ***Go to Section 3***

2.2 Do you *really* want to leave the gym? Because I've got to say, you look like you could use a little more work.

☐ Yes, I really want to leave the gym. ***Go to the next question***

☐ No, you're right. I'll keep coming back. ***Go to Section 3***

2.3 Have you heard the phrase 'winners never quit and quitters never win'?

☐ Yes, I've heard that and I still want to leave. ***Go to the next question***

☐ No, when you put it like that, I can see that I should probably stick it out. Thanks! ***Go to Section 3***

2.4 You do know that you won't be able to use our pool or new Swedish sauna, don't you?

☐ Yes, but I don't care. ***Go to the next question***

☐ No, I wouldn't want to miss out on those. I'll stay. ***Go to Section 3***

2.5 And you know that the gym is a great place to meet people, don't you? I mean, just look at all the good looking people here, getting sweaty and wearing spandex. Do you really want to turn your back on all those *fringe benefits*, if you know what I mean?

☐ Yes, I'm giving up the fringe benefits because I'm a timid little mouse. ***Go to the next question***

☐ No, thinking about it I could meet some great people here. I think I'll give it another go. ***Go to Section 3***

2.6 I don't want to scare you, but you know that lack of regular exercise increases your risk of heart disease and other fatal conditions, don't you?

☐ Yes, I know that and I still want to leave the gym. ***Go to the next question***

☐ No, I didn't know that. God, I'd better stick with it. ***Go to Section 3***

2.7 Did you know that studies have shown that people who regularly attend the gym are richer, happier and more sexually attractive than those that don't?

☐ Yes, but that's not going to stop me from leaving. ***Go to the next question***

☐ No, is that really true? Wow, I want to be one of those people. I'm staying. ***Go to Section 3***

2.8 Have you ever heard the saying 'winners never quit and quitters never win'?

- ☐ Yes, you already said that. It's still having no effect on me. ***Go to the next question***
- ☐ No. I mean yes, but I hadn't really *heard* it until now. Wow. That's really brought it into sharp focus. I've changed my mind. ***Go to Section 3***

2.9 Suppose someone breaks into your house? What if they threaten to hurt you, your kids or your partner? Are you just going to sit there and do nothing, impotently standing by because you're not physically fit enough to take on the burglar?

- ☐ Yes, I think the best thing to do would be cower in bed, or maybe hide in the cupboard and phone the police. Either way, I don't think confrontation would do any good in this kind of situation. Because, quite frankly, I'm a coward. ***Go to the next question***
- ☐ No, I'm too weak! I should come to the gym more and then I can protect myself and the things I care about. ***Go to Section 3***

2.10 So, you're caught in the middle of a siege between armed police and a terrorist splinter cell. After a bloody gun battle, all that's left is you, a bomb disposal expert and a explosive device that will disperse Anthrax spores across a hundred mile radius, killing everyone exposed to the bacteria. The disposal expert says that he can defuse the bomb, but he's going to need you to ride a stationary cycle to generate the electricity for his equipment. He says it'll take about twenty minutes and that the lives of millions of people depend on you being able to maintain an even speed of 15 mph without faltering. Are you going to risk all those lives just because you couldn't be bothered to get off your butt a few times a week?

- ☐ Yes. I'm willing to live with that. ***Go to next question***
- ☐ Noooooo! Please have me back. I don't want to be a mass murderer. ***Go to Section 3***

2.11 Finally, aliens come down from another planet and ask for mortal combat between their fiercest warrior and earth's greatest champion. Through a horrible series of accidents, you are selected as defender of the earth and you enter the arena to face down a slayer of unimaginable brutality, who has literally slaughtered entire worlds. Do you fancy your chances?

- ☐ Yes. Every dog has its day. ***Go to Section 4***
- ☐ No. I need to work on my abs, glutes and cardio in order to save the world. Sign me back up! ***Go to Section 3***

Section 3: Re-enrolment

3.1 Good for you. There's going to be a lot of people telling you that you've been bullied into staying, but don't listen to those losers. Just to make sure that you don't waver again in the future, how about we sign you up for a year's membership, paid in advance? You'll get a five percent discount and a free sports bag.

- ☐ Yes, I'll do whatever you tell me.

3.2 Great! Now, do 50 reps on the Nautilus and I'll see you in the showers. Good work, bud!

Section 4: Real quitters

4.1 Do you accept that you will be...?

- ☐ Flabby
- ☐ Saggy
- ☐ Wobbly
- ☐ Wheezy
- ☐ Ugly
- ☐ Cheesy

Tick them all. All of them.

4.2 Do you accept that you will NOT be...?

- ☐ Packed
- ☐ Ripped
- ☐ Jacked
- ☐ Cut
- ☐ Shredded
- ☐ Lean

Yes, I'm a lazy, shiftless, high-cholesterol, low-ambition, no-drive bottom feeder who just doesn't want to be trim, stacked or happy. I am quitting the gym and returning to my empty, saturated-fat lifestyle. I know it doesn't have to be like this, but I can't be arsed to do anything about it.

Signature .... **Date**...................

Permission to Create a Scene

Proper completion of this form entitles you to a special waiver, permitting you to kick up a stink in the specific circumstances you have outlined. Please note that said waiver will be limited to this particular date, time and location and is not a open licence to misbehave.

Section 1: Your details

1.1 Name

1.2 Date of birth

DD	MM	YYYY

1.4 Address

Section 2: Background information

2.1 Generally speaking, would you class yourself as…

- ☐ Hot-tempered
- ☐ Even-handed
- ☐ Passive

2.2 Would you say you lose your temper…

- ☐ Quickly
- ☐ Not very quickly
- ☐ Rarely

2.3 Have you ever created a scene before?

- ☐ Yes
- ☐ No

2.4 If YES, please indicate the frequency with which you create scenes

- ☐ Seldom (less than once a year)
- ☐ Sometimes (a few times a year)
- ☐ Regularly (every month or so)
- ☐ Constantly (every week)
- ☐ Endlessly (every day)
- ☐ It is my default state

2.5 Broadly speaking, which of the following trigger tempers, tantrums or scenes?

Tick all that apply

- ☐ Parking
- ☐ Traffic
- ☐ People who think they're it
- ☐ Waiters and waitresses
- ☐ Bureaucrats
- ☐ Nosy parkers
- ☐ Snobs
- ☐ Jobsworths
- ☐ Busybodies
- ☐ Vegans
- ☐ Posh people
- ☐ Common people
- ☐ Know-it-alls
- ☐ The wilfully ignorant
- ☐ Chelsea fans
- ☐ Misspelled words
- ☐ Grammar nazis
- ☐ Young people

Section 3: The Scene

3.1 Location of proposed outburst, ruckus or hullaballoo

3.2 Date and time of scene

DD MM YYYY at HH AM /PM

3.3 Duration of scene

☐ minute(s) ☐ hour(s) ☐ day(s)

3.4 The principle catalyst for the outburst will be

3.5 The majority of my fury will be directed at

3.6 Do you intend to damage and/or deface your surroundings when creating your scene?

- ☐ Yes
- ☐ No

3.7 If YES, please estimate the cash value of the damage you intend to cause

£

3.8 I would like to use the following words

- ☐ Bloody
- ☐ Effing
- ☐ Officious
- ☐ Outrageous
- ☐ Petty
- ☐ Scumbag
- ☐ Small-minded
- ☐ Stupid
- ☐ Tight-arsed
- ☐ Wrong

3.9 And these phrases

- ☐ It's not about the money
- ☐ It's the principle of the thing
- ☐ Don't talk to me like that
- ☐ No, I will not lower my voice
- ☐ That's what I've been trying to tell you
- ☐ Just listen for a moment, will you?
- ☐ Don't touch me
- ☐ He/she/they started it
- ☐ I'm perfectly calm
- ☐ Come on, be reasonable

3.11 During this scene, I will be accompanied by

- ☐ Spouse/partner
- ☐ Children
- ☐ Friend
- ☐ Colleague
- ☐ Parent
- ☐ Other

3.12 I expect them to be

- ☐ Slightly embarrassed
- ☐ Proud
- ☐ Ashamed
- ☐ Apologetic
- ☐ Crying
- ☐ Goading me on

3.14 If security and/or police are called, I will...

- ☐ Go quietly
- ☐ Kick up a fuss, but leave before things go too far
- ☐ Get physical
- ☐ Have to be dragged away, kicking and screaming

3.15 If the scene could be rectified with a simple apology, would you accept that as a suitable alternative and thereby avoid all the shouting and embarrassment?

- ☐ Yes
- ☐ No, I have my principles and I'm not compromising them for you or anybody

OK, I've filled out your stupid little form, you paper-pushing jobsworth. Is there anything else you want from me?
A pound of flesh, maybe, or my firstborn child?
Take your poxy form and stick it where the sun don't shine.

Signature .... **Date** ....

Permission to Riot

Riots are spontaneous explosions of civil unrest that occur when the usual rules of society have broken down. Ensure that you have fully completed this form in order to obtain the express permission of the relevant authorities for your explosion of disorder.

Section 1: Causes and instigators

1.1 Main Instigator

1.2 Secondary instigators / rabble-rousers

Please provide details of six other people who are involved in starting the riot.

1.	4.
2.	5.
3.	6.

1.3 Date and time when riot will begin

DD	MM	YYYY	at	HH	MM	AM / PM

1.4 Date and time when riot will end

DD	MM	YYYY	at	HH	MM	AM / PM

1.5 Proposed site of riot

Indicate where the riot will start and where you intend it to spread to.
Be as precise as possible, allowing for the indeterminate nature of disorganised protest.

1.6 Briefly describe the events and circumstances that have led up to this riot

e.g. 'The unlawful arrest of Peter Samson', 'Continuing abuse of stop and search powers' or 'Sold out of cronuts'.

Section 2: Scale

2.1 Category of event

- ☐ Scuffle
- ☐ Skirmish
- ☐ Fracas
- ☐ Melee
- ☐ Conflict
- ☐ Riot
- ☐ Total breakdown of law and order
- ☐ Collapse of civilisation

2.2 Estimated number of rioters

2.3 Estimated number of people that are NOT rioters, but caught up in the event

Section 3: Riot details

3.1 Main focus of aggression

- ☐ Business
- ☐ Government
- ☐ Law Enforcement
- ☐ Judiciary
- ☐ Economic institution
- ☐ Educational institution

3.2 Property targeted during riot

- ☐ Local businesses
- ☐ Police station
- ☐ Local amenities
- ☐ Transport
- ☐ Council property
- ☐ Homes

3.3 Estimated value of property damage

£

3.4 Estimated number of casualties

	Minor injuries	Serious injuries	Fatalities
Rioters			
Bystanders			
Police			
Other emergency workers			

3.5 Estimated number of arrests

3.6 Percentage of which will be wrongful

%

3.7 Signature chants

e.g. "No Justice, No Peace!", "Free Delroy Lindo", etc.

Section 4: Riot response

4.1 Measures that will need to be deployed in response to your riot

- ☐ Volunteer stewards
- ☐ Uniformed police officers
- ☐ Riot police
- ☐ Army soldiers
- ☐ Tear gas
- ☐ Water cannon
- ☐ Rubber bullets
- ☐ Combat batons
- ☐ Full artillery

4.2 Predicted response of general public to your riot

- ☐ Sympathetic
- ☐ Apathetic
- ☐ Apoplectic

As a duly appointed representative of the lawless mob described above, I hereby apply to the relevant authorities for permission to duly ignore their authority and act in accordance with no generally recognised understanding of the rule of law.

In the event of the riot escalating beyond the criteria outlined in this form, I understand that I may be called on to advise on the anarchistic collective that rises from the ashes.

Signature .... **Date** ....

Planning Permission Request (Hard Water Nuclear Reactor)

Failure to properly submit the application may result in a fine, seizure of materials by the Local Authority and a formal censure from the United Nations.

Section 1: Applicant Details

1.1 Title

- ☐ Mr
- ☐ Mrs
- ☐ Ms
- ☐ Doctor
- ☐ Professor
- ☐ General
- ☐ Sir
- ☐ Archbishop
- ☐ Chairman
- ☐ Prime Minister
- ☐ Supreme Leader
- ☐ El Presidente

1.2 Forename

1.3 Surname

1.4 Tick the highest level of scientific / engineering qualification you have attained

- ☐ PhD
- ☐ Masters
- ☐ Undergraduate degree
- ☐ A-Level / HND
- ☐ BTEC / NVQ
- ☐ GCSE
- ☐ O-Level
- ☐ Primary school 'Buster Brainbox' certificate

Section 2: Proposed reactor site

2.1 Address of proposed site

2.2 Type of building in which reactor is to be housed:

- ☐ Detached house
- ☐ Semi-detached house
- ☐ Terraced house
- ☐ Flat
- ☐ Office
- ☐ Shop
- ☐ Lockup
- ☐ Garage
- ☐ Shed
- ☐ Other

2.3 Who will be responsible for maintaining security of the reactor site, both during construction and when it is operational?

- ☐ Private security firm
- ☐ State armed forces / militia
- ☐ Civilian police force
- ☐ Neighbourhood watch

2.4 Have you notified your neighbours of your intent to construct a hard-water reactor and obtained their consent to go ahead?

- ☐ Yes
- ☐ No

2.5 Have you placed a notice in the local paper of your intent to apply for permission to construct a hard-water reactor?

- ☐ Yes
- ☐ No

Section 3: Reactor details

3.1 Name of reactor
(e.g. Daisybank, Project Smiling Buddha, Joybringer, etc.)

3.2 Principle use for reactor
- ☐ Domestic energy needs
- ☐ Selling energy on the international market
- ☐ Creating plutonium and tritium for nuclear weapons
- ☐ Hobby / DIY project

3.3 Please give your estimated annual output in MegaWatts(electrical)

	MWe per annum

3.4 How many people do you estimate will be needed to *safely* run the reactor?
- ☐ 1-9
- ☐ 10-49
- ☐ 50-250
- ☐ 250+

3.5 Where will you be getting the uranium required for your reactor?
- ☐ The international market
- ☐ The black market
- ☐ A dismantled nuclear weapon
- ☐ I will mine it myself

3.6 Please indicate your proposed storage facility for uranium and other fissile materials
- ☐ Lead containers placed within concrete enclosure no less than 6 inches thick
- ☐ Hermetically sealed steel chamber
- ☐ Tupperware
- ☐ Thermos flask

3.7 How will you be disposing of the hazardous by-products of your hard-water reactor?
- ☐ In strict accordance with IAEA guidelines
- ☐ Selling them to terrorists, so they can build a dirty bomb
- ☐ Landfill
- ☐ Wheelie bin

3.8 How will you be funding the construction of your nuclear reactor?
- ☐ Bank loan
- ☐ Local terrorist group
- ☐ Grant from a foreign government, namely:________________________________
- ☐ Independent fundraising (raffle, bakesale, etc.)

3.9 Have you enclosed the application processing fee of £1,250,000?
- ☐ Yes
- ☐ No
- ☐ I'll have to pay you in installments

I declare that the information I have given in this form is, to the best of my knowledge, complete, honest and accurate. I understand that failure to properly co-operate with regulatory authorities or UN inspectors can lead to sanctions and/or more extreme measures. Please don't bomb me.

Signature .... **Date** ....

Proposal for a New Alphabet

The Language Advisory Council is now accepting submissions for a new, improved alphabet. Applications will be reviewed by a panel of experts and the successful applicant will have a dictionary named in their honour.

Section 1: Your new alphabet

1.1 Please provide your new uppercase and lowercase letterforms in the spaces provided, matching them to the traditional letters

A	B	C	D	E	F	G	H	I	J
a	b	c	d	e	f	g	h	i	j
K	L	M	N	O	P	Q	R	S	T
k	l	m	n	o	p	q	r	s	t
U	V	X	Y	Z	.	,	?	!	"
u	v	x	y	z	(	)	&	/	'

1.2 Please provide your new numbers, from 0 to 9 in the spaces provided, matching them to their traditional counterparts

0	1	2	3	4	5	6	7	8	9

1.3 Print your full name, using your new proposed alphabet

1.4 Print the following well known phrase, using your proposed new alphabet

T	h	e		q	u	i	c	k		b	r	o	w	n		f	o	x		j	u	m	p	e	d

o	v	e	r		t	h	e		l	a	z	y		d	o	g	.

Section 2: About your new alphabet

2.1 New alphabet name

2.2 Give details of your influences / inspiration for the design of the letters

2.3 Briefly explain the advantages you feel your new alphabet has over the current one

Section 3: Applicant details

3.1 Name

3.2 Address

3.3 Occupation

3.4 Date of birth

DD	MM	YYYY

3.5 Have you ever designed an alphabet or code cypher before?

☐ Yes
☐ No

3.6 If YES, for whom?

☐ Government
☐ Intelligence agency
☐ Fantasy novel or role playing game
☐ Other professional capacity
☐ Just for fun

I hereby certify that the alphabet provided in this application is entirely my own work and not copied from any other sources.

Signature (in English) .... **Date (standard numbers)** ....

Provisional License to Kill

A Provisional Licence to Kill intended for trainee agents of Her Majesty's Secret Service to gain experience in the deadly arts and further your repertoire of inhuman banter. A provisional licence to kill allows you to take lives in the course of duty, but only when accompanied by a fully licenced killer (except on private roads and thoroughfares).

Section 1: Your application

1.1 Surname

1.2 Forename Surname

1.3 Codename

1.4 Date of Birth

DD	MM	YYYY

1.5 Department

1.6 Have you killed anyone prior to making this application ?

Failure to disclose previous fatalities could result in rejection, prosecution and exciting 'agent gone rogue' storylines

☐ Yes
☐ No

1.7 If YES, please give details (use additional sheet if required)

Section 2: Basic Skills

2.1 List in order of preference your preferred weapons (1= favourite, 10 = least favourite)

Firearms		Laser pen	
Explosives		Umbrella with a poison tip	
Hand-to-hand combat		Radioactive cufflinks	
Knives / Edged weapons		Hypnotic suggestion, leading to suicide	
Concealed gas pellets		Alligator	

2.2 You have just pushed a man into an industrial sausage press.
Once you've watched him fall to his doom and you have straightened your tie, what do you say?

2.3 A woman has attempted to strangle you with a pair of silk stockings.
Once you have escaped her clutches and killed her, what do you say?

2.4 Match these enemies to the most effective and/or appropriate means of disposal

Draw lines to connect the enemy and method of death

Diminutive Japanese geisha with razor-tipped fans	o	o	Burned to death in super-hot greenhouse
Australian media mogul looking to control world events in order to consolidate his media monopoly	o	o	Drowned in oil well
Ex-KGB officer attempting to crash world stock market in order to instigate worldwide Communist revolution	o	o	Sliced into sushi-sized chunks by air conditioning unit
Swiss botanist who has genetically engineered a strain of poppy that produces cheap, pure heroin	o	o	Crushed by giant satellite dish
Arab Sheik who will blow up rival nations in order to control world oil market	o	o	Trampled to death by enthusiastic traders

2.5 You have detained an enemy henchman for questioning. On the diagram below, mark three points where you can inflict a non-fatal wound in order to convince him to talk. Mark these 1, 2 and 3 to indicate your first, second and third wound, be they actual or intended, then describe the wounds in the adjacent column.

1

2

3

Section 3: References

3.1 Circle your commanding officer and/or any personal referees

A	B	C	D	E	F	G	H	I	J	K	L	M
N	O	P	Q	R	S	T	U	V	W	X	Y	Z

I hereby swear that the information I have provided is honest, accurate and complete. Should it later emerge that the information I have given is proven false, I accept that I may be subject to disciplinary action, criminal prosecution, dismissal from HMSS and that I may be strapped to a table while a white-hot laser inches ever closer to my genitals.

Signature .... **Date**...................

Pro Wrestler Registration

Professional Wrestling is on the upswing and there are well-paid opportunities for people willing to undergo the rigorous training and gruelling schedule. If you're looking to launch a career injuring yourself by pretending to hurt others, please complete this form in full.

Section 1: Your details

1.1 Real Name

[ ]

1.2 Ring name

[ ]

1.3 Hailing from

This should reflect your persona. For example, a body builder would come from Muscle Beach, USA. An intelligent grappler would be from Cambridge, England, etc.

[ ]

1.4 Weight

	lb

1.5 Height

Add at least four inches to your real height

	feet		inches

Section 2: Your character

2.1 Orientation

Broadly speaking, whether you are a hero or villain. Note that this will be liable to many, many changes over time.

☐ Face (good) ☐ Heel (bad) ☐ Tweener (bit of both)

2.2 Wrestling style

☐ Brawler
☐ Technical athlete
☐ High flyer
☐ Dirty fighter
☐ Monster hoss
☐ Insane risk-taker

2.3 Source of your abilities

☐ Natural athleticism
☐ Tutelage by wrestling legend
☐ Martial arts training
☐ Millions of dollars
☐ Demonic forces
☐ Steroids

2.4 Will your character be based around a culturally insensitive stereotype?

You do not have to use a culturally insensitive stereotype, but it may harm your chances of success if you do not.

☐ Yes
☐ No

2.5 If YES, please give details here

[ ]

Section 3: Knowledge of the business

3.1 Are you smart?

- ☐ Yes
- ☐ No
- ☐ I don't understand the question

3.2 Match the industry terminology to its proper definition

Shoot	o	o	Popular
Kayfabe	o	o	Real
Over	o	o	Fan
Mark	o	o	Storyline
Bump	o	o	Blood
Pop	o	o	Move
Colour	o	o	Fall
Spot	o	o	Cheer

Section 4: Management

4.1 Will you be requiring the services of a manager?

You may want a manager if you do not feel confident talking yourself up and/or your opponent down.

- ☐ Yes
- ☐ No

4.2 If YES, what type?

- ☐ Eye candy
- ☐ Shrieking harridan
- ☐ Slimy executive
- ☐ Academic professor
- ☐ Sports coach
- ☐ Mystical shaman
- ☐ Funeral director
- ☐ Pimp

Section 5: Promotion

5.1 Please indicate which of the following you would NOT be willing to do to promote a wrestling match

- ☐ Take the lord's name in vain
- ☐ Threaten a member of the opposite sex
- ☐ Nudity and/or sexual activity
- ☐ Be covered in manure / oil / tar
- ☐ Incite racial animosity
- ☐ Depict an incestuous relationship
- ☐ Utter homophobic slurs
- ☐ None of the above – I want to be a pro wrestler

5.2 Please provide a short promo for an upcoming event called Slam Jam where you will be wrestling an opponent called 'The Phantom'

I hereby submit my application to be a pro wrestler, knowing full well that it will likely result in debilitating physical injury, psychological trauma, social ostracism and narcotic dependance. I understand that even if I am to be successful, my pursuit of this dream means I will be unable to hold a regular job again and will spend my dotage fighting tranquilized bears in high school gymnasiums.

Signature .... **Date** ....

Quick and Easy Voodoo

The dark magic of voodoo used to be the sole preserve of witchdoctors and wise women, but no longer! Nowadays, putting a hex on someone doesn't require slaughtering chickens or burying bones. With just a pen and paper, you too can do the hoodoo!

Section 1: About you

1.1 Name

[ ]

1.2 Have you ever engaged in any of the following activities?

- ☐ Seance
- ☐ Incantation
- ☐ Necromancy
- ☐ Astral projection
- ☐ Possession
- ☐ Summoning a demon, devil or dybbuk

Section 2: The hex

2.1 Name of Hexee

[ ]

2.2 Hexee's relationship to you

- ☐ Friend
- ☐ Colleague
- ☐ Partner
- ☐ Ex-partner
- ☐ Relative
- ☐ Rival
- ☐ Stranger

2.3 Type of hex you wish to place on them

Hexes can be both positive and negative, depending on your actions

- ☐ Sex hex
- ☐ Love hex
- ☐ Job hex
- ☐ Health hex
- ☐ Money hex
- ☐ Pain hex

2.4 Explain why you want to put a hex on this person

[ ]

2.5 Do you want your power over this person to be

- ☐ Permanent
- ☐ Temporary

If temporary, specify approximate time period

[ ]

Section 3: The doll

Each section of the figure will have a different effect on the hexee. Put a tick or a cross on the parts of the figure you wish to affect in your hexee.

Head
Cross – Cause headaches
Tick – Stimulate thinking

Mouth
Cross – Strike mute
Tick – Speak wisely

Eyes
Cross – Cause blindness
Tick – See clearly

Ears
Cross – Hear only falsehoods
Tick – Listen and understand

Right Hand
Cross – Lose possessions
Tick – Gain friends

Left Hand
Cross – Start fights
Tick – Mend divisions

Heart
Cross – Break heart
Tick – Find love

Stomach
Cross – Go hungry
Tick – Know warmth

Groin
Cross – Urinary problems
Tick – Great sex

Left Knee
Cross – Beg for mercy
Tick – Grant forgiveness

Right Knee
Cross – Neglect family
Tick – Raise children

Feet
Cross – Isolation
Tick – Travel

Yes, I understand that I am meddling with powerful spirits that I cannot properly comprehend and that the spirits ask a terrible price of those who attempt to control them.
That said, I'm sure it'll all work out fine in the end.

Signature .... **Date** ....

Register a New Religion

Faith is a wonderful thing. With many of history's greatest problems being caused by religious disagreements, it's time for newer, smarter, better religions. If you think you've got the answers, or if you're just looking for some people to boss around, register your new religion today.

Section 1: Your new religion

1.1 Applicant name

1.2 What is your role in this new religion?

- ☐ Humble practitioner
- ☐ Congregation leader
- ☐ Evangelist
- ☐ Religious Icon
- ☐ Head of church
- ☐ Deity

1.3 Name of new religion

1.4 Who or what do you worship?

1.5 Please draw a symbol that identifies your new religion.

(It is recommended to keep it simple for easy identification. Think ✞✡☪)

1.6 Briefly explain what your religion offers that others do not

1.7 List three (3) key things that your religion advocates

1.
2.
3.

1.8 List three (3) key things that your religion forbids

1.
2.
3.

Section 2: Dogma and Heresy

2.1 Categorise your new religion's stance on the following issues

	For	Against	No opinion
Contraception	☐	☐	☐
Homosexuality	☐	☐	☐
Interfaith relationships	☐	☐	☐
Evolution	☐	☐	☐
Alcohol	☐	☐	☐
Drugs	☐	☐	☐
Sex before marriage	☐	☐	☐
Abortion	☐	☐	☐
Women	☐	☐	☐

Section 3: Rituals and practices

3.1 Please outline the basic daily routine that followers of your religion will be expected to practice

Upon waking	
During the day	
At night	
Before going to sleep	

3.2 Please give details of anything that followers of your religion will be expected to forgo

3.3 Please give details of any specific clothing associated with your new religion
e.g. yarmulke, turban, burkha, etc.

3.4 If your religion has a holy book or official scripture, please name it here

3.5 According to your religion, what happens to people when they die?

As a faithful practitioner of this new faith, I humbly submit this document for approval by a higher power, whether that be God, the Universe, humanity at large or just the public affairs office of the local council. Amen.

Signature .... **Date** ....

Report of a Break-In

Burglary rates are on the rise, but we are constantly striving to improve not only the quantity, but also the quality of our break-ins. Please take this opportunity to complete this form and assist us in improving our service.

Section 1: Your details

1.1 Name

☐

1.2 Address of property broken in to

1.3 Nature of premises

- ☐ Office
- ☐ Shop
- ☐ House
- ☐ Flat
- ☐ Maisonette
- ☐ Bungalow
- ☐ Stately home
- ☐ Yacht

1.4 Nature of tenancy

- ☐ Homeowner
- ☐ Tenant
- ☐ Staying with family

1.5 How long have you lived/worked in these premises?

	Months		Years

Section 2: What was taken

2.1 Please indicate which items were taken

- ☐ TV
- ☐ Stereo
- ☐ DVD Player
- ☐ Games console
- ☐ Computer
- ☐ Mobile phone
- ☐ Camera
- ☐ Camcorder
- ☐ Jewellery
- ☐ Clothing
- ☐ Cash
- ☐ Credit / Debit / Store cards
- ☐ Refrigerator
- ☐ Washing Machine
- ☐ Boiler
- ☐ Car
- ☐ Motorcycle
- ☐ Caravan
- ☐ Bicycle
- ☐ Fitness equipment
- ☐ Cindy Crawford Workout Video
- ☐ Family pet
- ☐ Wheelie bin
- ☐ Garden Shed
- ☐ Windows
- ☐ Doors
- ☐ Underwear
- ☐ Homemade pornography
- ☐ Children's toys
- ☐ Children

2.2 Please list any additional items, not mentioned on the list above

2.3 Please list any additional items not mentioned on the list above, which you did not actually own, but intend to claim for on the insurance

Section 3: Value of what was taken

3.1 Of the items we took, would you say most of them were of...

☐ Financial Value
☐ Sentimental Value
☐ Equal financial and sentimental value

3.2 Estimated financial value of stolen items

£

3.3 What was the most valuable item we took?

3.4 What was the most valuable item we missed?

3.5 Are there any items that the burglars did not take, but that you wish they had? If so, please list below.

Section 4: Our staff

4.1 Were you in when our agents visited your premises?

☐ Yes
☐ No

4.2 If YES, how much noise did they make?

☐ None – we remained oblivious to their presence
☐ Some – we heard something, but didn't think anything of it
☐ Lots – we were terrified

4.3 If you had been aware of our team's presence in your property,do you think you would have confronted them?

☐ Yes ☐ No ☐ Not sure

4.4 Did we provide any of the following additional services?

We believe that burglary is about more than just taking items from your home. Hopefully, our agents have provided you with a complete service. Please tick all the boxes that apply in your case.

☐ Big poo in the toilet
☐ Big poo elsewhere
☐ Food eaten
☐ Family pet shaved / spray-painted
☐ Underwear drawer rummaged
☐ Moustaches drawn on to photographs
☐ Answerphone message changed
☐ Freezer left to defrost
☐ Taps left running
☐ Fish in the airing cupboard

4.5 Did we leave your place...?

☐ Utterly ransacked ☐ A bit messy ☐ Better than before

4.6 Overall, how do you feel after the break-in?

☐ Completely violated ☐ A bit shaken up ☐ Over the moon

Return this survey within seven days of your burglary and we'll send you a free picture of your toothbrush being used in a disgustingly creative manner.

Signature .... **Date** ....

Repossession Notice

This form may be used by you (the *claimant*) to give notice to a friend, relative or colleague of your intention to take back an item that they have borrowed from you. This person (the *current possessor*) will have the right to respond in Section 2, overleaf.

Section 1: To be completed by the claimant

1.1 Claimant surname

1.2 Claimant forename(s)

1.3 Item(s) to be repossessed

1.4 Monetary value of item(s)

£

☐ Tick here if it's not about the money, it's the principle of the thing

1.5 Date when said items left your possession

DD MM YYYY

1.6 Current possessor surname

1.7 Current possessor forename(s)

1.8 Relationship to you

☐ Friend
☐ Relative
☐ Colleague
☐ Acquaintance
☐ Partner / Spouse
☐ Other

1.9 Has anyone else had possession of the item(s)?

☐ Yes
☐ No

Give their name here

1.10 Briefly summarise how the item(s) left your possession and how they came to the current possessor

1.11 Write a brief statement to the current possessor, explaining why you are repossessing the item(s)

I assert that I have a rightful claim to the item(s) in question and that all information provided is truthful and accurate, to the best of my knowledge.

Claimant signature ....

Date ....

Section 2: To be completed by the current possessor

2.1 Do you still have the item(s) in question?
☐ Yes (go to **2.5**)
☐ No

2.2 If NO, where is it / are they?

☐ Don't know

2.3 Can you get it / them back?
☐ Yes
☐ No
☐ I can, but I won't

2.4 Compensation to be offered in lieu of item(s)

☐ None

2.5 Will you return the item(s) named in Question 1.3?
☐ Yes (go to **2.6**)
☐ No (go to **2.7**)
☐ Some of them (go to **2.8**)

2.6 If YES, you may use this space to explain why you had the item(s) in the first place.
You may also use this space to apologise, but do not have to do so if you do not want to.

2.7 If NO, please categorise your reasons for not returning said item(s)
Tick all that apply. You may use the box below for any additional reasons and/or supporting information
☐ It's mine
☐ I paid for it
☐ It was given to me
☐ They don't take care of it
☐ They don't deserve it
☐ It was mine originally

Additional notes

2.8 If SOME to Question 2.5, please explain what happened and why the complete item(s) cannot be returned

2.9 Categorise the events that led up to you having the item(s) in your possession
☐ A big misunderstanding
☐ A situation that spiralled out of control
☐ Luck of the draw
☐ Just desserts

I have read and understood the claimant's repossession as outlined in Section 1 and have made my feelings on the subject quite clear. As far as I'm concerned, this situation has been put to rest.

Possessor signature .... **Date**...................

School of Hard Knocks Postgraduate Registration

This form is intended for those seeking further study at the School of Hard Knocks. Postgraduate study is multidisciplinary and requires exceptional levels of rigour.

Section 1: Student details

1.1 Name

1.2 Date of birth

DD	MM	YYYY

1.3 Address

If you do not have a address, put down the last place you slept

1.4 Please indicate if you have any of the following qualifications

While the following are not prerequisites for entry into the School of Hard Knocks postgraduate programme, they will give us a better understanding of your experience.

- ☐ Criminal record
- ☐ Physical disability
- ☐ Mental disability
- ☐ Addiction issues
- ☐ Sexual abuse
- ☐ Traumatic upbringing
- ☐ Family separation
- ☐ Racism
- ☐ Sexism
- ☐ Homophobia
- ☐ Transphobia
- ☐ Exposure to adult behaviour at early age
- ☐ Torture (physical or mental)
- ☐ Bullying
- ☐ Eating disorder
- ☐ Self-harm
- ☐ Mood disorder
- ☐ Psychosis
- ☐ Chronic pain

1.5 Next of kin

Many of our students do not have next of kin, however we are legally required to notify someone in the event of accident, injury or death. Please provide indications as to who we might be able to inform.

	No, dead	No, missing	No, in prison	No, In hospital	No, inebriated	No, mental	No, toxic	Maybe
Mother	☐	☐	☐	☐	☐	☐	☐	☐
Father	☐	☐	☐	☐	☐	☐	☐	☐
Grandmother	☐	☐	☐	☐	☐	☐	☐	☐
Grandfather	☐	☐	☐	☐	☐	☐	☐	☐
Brother	☐	☐	☐	☐	☐	☐	☐	☐
Sister	☐	☐	☐	☐	☐	☐	☐	☐
Spouse/Partner	☐	☐	☐	☐	☐	☐	☐	☐
Son	☐	☐	☐	☐	☐	☐	☐	☐
Daughter	☐	☐	☐	☐	☐	☐	☐	☐
Social worker	☐	☐	☐	☐	☐	☐	☐	☐
Parole officer	☐	☐	☐	☐	☐	☐	☐	☐

1.6 How long do you intend to study with us?

- ☐ 1 year
- ☐ 2 years
- ☐ 3 years
- ☐ Indefinitely

Section 2: Your syllabus

The School of Hard Knocks post-graduate programme allows you to study in a variety of Faculties, in order to fully enable your education. Please choose from the courses below and title your course at the bottom of the page.

Faculty of Chemistry	Faculty of Human Affairs	Faculty of Economics	Faculty of Law
CH8050 Cannaboid Lifestyles **CH9090** Advanced Alcoholism **CH4010** Running a Crackhouse **CH6030** Prescription Procurement and Forgery **CH4260** Opiates Today **CH5420** Further Meths	**HU5550** Sustaining Abusive Relationships **HU6460** Intergenerational Pederasty **HU9010** Why He Will Never Leave Her **HU4070** Beyond the Restraining Order **HU9090** Online Abuse and Social Networking **HU2260** My Family Can Never Know	**EC8090** Payday Loans **EC6720** Effective Begging Strategies **EC7810** Coming to Some Arrangement With Debtors **EC4040** Benefit Sanctions **EC5010** Luxury Shoplifting **EC4010** Food Banking	**LW7720** Falling Out of the Van **LW4540** A Suspect Matching Your Description **LW6820** A Case Study in Judicial Bias Against You **LW9030** Repossession **LW3010** Keeping Schtum **LA5040** Becoming a Habitual Offender
Faculty of Zoology	Faculty of Inhumanities	Faculty of Psychiatry	Faculty of Art
ZO5620 Loan sharks **ZO8280** Sexual Predators **ZO7010** The Virus Inside You **ZO3420** Bitches and Dogs **ZO4040** Parasitic Relationships **ZO2090** Scabies, Rabies and Babies	**IH5020** Reliving War Crimes **IH5270** PTSD Every Day **IH7010** Hostages in the Home **IH6050** Human Trafficking **IH6060** Sex Tourism **IH4280** Child Brides	**PS5020** The Shadow People **PS3020** Going Off Meds **PS5710** Messages From Your Pets **PS4910** How Everyone You Know is Communicating With Each Other **PS8330** What Was That? **PS3070** Sectioning	**AR5010** Forging Signatures **AR4220** After Pollock – Vomit and Faecal Spray **AR3040** Caught on CCTV – Video Performance in the 21st Century **AR6070** Dancing in Traffic **AR2090** Compromising Photography **AR8750** Your Music 'Career'

2.1 Please select eight (8) courses that will make up your first year programme.
Use the course codes listed above. Your programme can be made up of courses from any Faculty.

2.2 Please select two (2) backup choices, just in case your first choices are not available
While every effort is made to fulfil first choice options, scheduling conflicts or oversubscription may mean that a course is unavailable. Please don't take this the wrong way and please do not threaten our staff.

2.3 Please give a title to your post-graduate programme
For example, 'Advanced Diploma in Drug-Related Crime' or 'Doctor of Thuganomics'.

I have completed my registration document in full and hereby submit my application for Postgraduate study at the School of Hard Knocks.

Signature .... **Date** ....

Seance-by-Mail

Try to relax and clear your mind while your psychic attempts to get in touch with the spirit world. The spiritual process is a mysterious and unpredictable phenomenon. Results may vary.

Section 1: Your details

1.1 Your name

[ ]

1.2 Date of birth

DD	MM	YYYY

1.3 Current bank balance

£

1.4 With regards to the spirit world, would you say you are…

☐ A believer
☐ A sceptic
☐ Undecided

Section 2: Your reading

2.1 You were close to this person, weren't you?

☐ Yes
☐ No

2.2 And you miss them, don't you?

☐ Yes
☐ No

2.3 Do the letters J and maybe an M mean anything to you?

☐ Yes
☐ No

2.4 What about G and B?

☐ Yes
☐ No

2.5 I'm getting the sense that this is an older person – someone who had a strong influence on your life. Do you know who that might be?

☐ Yes
☐ No

2.6 They're saying that the two of you didn't always get on, but they want you to know that they always loved you. Does that make sense?

☐ Yes
☐ No

2.7 I'm getting an image of a house… a place where you felt safe. Do you know the place I'm talking about?

☐ Yes
☐ No

2.8 You sometimes think about the times you spent there with this person, don't you?

☐ Yes
☐ No

2.9 They want you to know that they remember, too. They haven't forgotten. Does that make sense to you?
☐ Yes
☐ No

2.10 You've got a box full of unsorted photographs in a room at home, haven't you?
☐ Yes
☐ No

2.11 They want you to look through them and remember the good times. Can you do that for them?
☐ Yes
☐ No

2.12 You've made some mistakes in your life, haven't you?
☐ Yes
☐ No

2.13 And even though you've managed to get past them, you still find yourself thinking about them, don't you?
☐ Yes
☐ No

2.14 You feel guilty sometimes, don't you?
☐ Yes
☐ No

2.15 They're telling me that you shouldn't be so hard on yourself. They know you did your best and it doesn't change the way they feel about you. Do you understand?
☐ Yes
☐ No

2.16 They say they've been watching you and they're proud of you. They love you and they'll always love you and as long as you don't forget them, they'll never leave you. Will you promise to remember them?
☐ Yes
☐ No

2.17 They're saying that they're happy where they are. They're not in any pain any more. Do you understand that?
☐ Yes
☐ No

2.18 Do you feel better now?
☐ Yes
☐ No

If YES, do it again, whenever you need.
If NO, you probably weren't trying hard enough. Do it again, whenever you need.

Section 3: Payment details

☐ Visa ☐ Mastercard ☐ American Express ☐ Switch/Maestro

Amount payable	£											
Cardholder name												
Card number												
Expiry date	/				CVC code							
Start date	/				Issue no.							
Signature												

Sell Your Soul

Selling your soul used to involve pentagrams, incantations and lengthy one-on-one negotiations with a demon. Spiritual deregulation means we can now process your transaction quickly and easily, so you could be enjoying the benefits of your deal in a fraction of the time. We take virtually any old soul, no matter how tainted it may be.

Section 1: You and your soul

1.1 Name

1.2 Date of birth

DD	MM	YYYY

1.3 Religious denomination

- ☐ Agnostic
- ☐ Atheist
- ☐ Christian
- ☐ Hindu
- ☐ Jain
- ☐ Jewish
- ☐ Muslim
- ☐ Sikh
- ☐ Other

1.4 Have you ever tried to sell your soul before?

Failure to disclose previous transactions may result in criminal prosecution and/or eternal damnation

- ☐ Yes
- ☐ No

If YES, please give details, including the counteroffer and date of negotiation

1.5 Have you had your soul professionally appraised by a cleric, shaman or licensed pawnbroker?

- ☐ Yes
- ☐ No

If YES, briefly explain why you did not sell your soul at that time

1.6 How would you best describe the condition of your soul?

This is for initial categorisation purposes only. A professional evaluator will assess your soul and categorise it for you.

- ☐ Immaculate
- ☐ Good
- ☐ Fair
- ☐ Poor
- ☐ Catastrophic

1.7 What would you like to exchange your soul for? TICK ONE ONLY

- ☐ I would like to exchange my soul for a cash lump sum — **Go to Section 2**
- ☐ I would like a specific service in exchange for my soul— **Go to Section 3**

Section 2: Soul for Cash

2.1 How much do you think your soul is worth?

£

2.2 What do you intend to use the money for?

- ☐ New car
- ☐ Holiday
- ☐ Home improvements
- ☐ Setting up a small business
- ☐ Investments
- ☐ Debts
- ☐ Drugs
- ☐ Sex
- ☐ Other

Section 3: Soul for Services

3.1 Please tick the boxes below to indicate what service you would like
Tick one box from each column
I would like for...

☐ Me	☐ …to kill…	☐ A withered penis
☐ My partner	☐ …to have…	☐ A large pile of money
☐ The world	☐ …to fall in love with…	☐ Oil
☐ My children	☐ …to never run out of…	☐ The Prime Minister
☐ My next door neighbour	☐ …to rub Vaseline into…	☐ God
☐ My ex	☐ …to be promoted to…	☐ A Greggs sausage roll
☐ My mother	☐ …to have an argument with…	☐ A gorilla
☐ My father	☐ …to become…	☐ Rabid marsupials
☐ My employer	☐ …to turn into…	☐ Syphilis
☐ My co-workers	☐ …to eat…	☐ 3 tonnes of concrete
☐ A random stranger	☐ …to be eaten by…	☐ A very big sandwich
☐ The winner of 'The Great British Bake-Off'	☐ ..to make a pornographic film with…	☐ The Isle of Wight
☐ The cast of 'Hollyoaks'	☐ …to bare-knuckle fight…	☐ A 1st edition of 'Edwin Drood'
☐ A member of the Royal Family	☐ …to emerge victorious from…	☐ Two Polynesian dwarves
☐ That foxy barista	☐ …to head-butt…	☐ My local MP
☐ The landlord at my local pub	☐ …to publicly condemn…	☐ Potty training
☐ A dachsund	☐ …to be caught lying to…	☐ An unceasing sense of dread
☐ Clive from accounts	☐ …to smoke weed with…	☐ The fattest dog in the world
☐ My PE teacher from school	☐ …to mud wrestle…	☐ 'Britain's Got Talent'
☐ That kid with the face	☐ …to dance the Macarena with…	☐ a dead badger in a lay-by
☐ That person I secretly fancy, but never speak to	☐ …to utterly humiliate…	☐ Leeds town centre
☐ That person I always speak to, but secretly hate	☐ …to be cured of…	☐ Purgatory
☐ My arch-enemy	☐ …to bathe in…	☐ Audaciously sexual lemurs
☐ My GP	☐ …to be infected with…	☐ Me
☐ Other (specify below)	☐ Other (specify below)	☐ Other (specify below)

Please note that personalised options may take longer to process and may require additional collateral on the part of the applicant, including the souls of children both born and unborn.

I hereby revoke my earthly soul and place it in the possession of the great lord Satan and his financial advisers.
I understand that this agreement is binding, unbreakable and irreversible.

Signature in blood.................................... **Date**....................

Shirk Permit

A Shirk Permit allows you to avoid your responsibilities in a certain area of your life. It is applicable only to the area you specify and is not a catch-all solution. Complete the form in full. Your application will be dealt with when we get around to it.

Section 1: Personal details

1.1 Name

1.2 Date of birth

DD	MM	YYYY

1.3 Relationship status

- ☐ Single
- ☐ In a relationship (under a year)
- ☐ Long term relationship
- ☐ Married / Civil partnership
- ☐ Divorced
- ☐ Widowed

Section 2: Your shirking life

2.1 How would you rank your rate of contribution, overall, in all areas of your life?

- ☐ I'm a grafter
- ☐ I do my bit
- ☐ About average
- ☐ There's no point busting a gut
- ☐ Anything for an easy life

2.2 Please indicate the general area in which you are seeking permission to shirk:

- ☐ Childcare
- ☐ Civic responsibility
- ☐ Domestic duties
- ☐ Family
- ☐ Financial
- ☐ Friendship
- ☐ Organisational role
- ☐ Personal relationship (partner / spouse)
- ☐ Studies
- ☐ Travel
- ☐ Work
- ☐ Other

2.3 Please give a brief account of which specific areas you are looking to slack off in

e.g. 'Taking my kids to school,' 'Cleaning up my dog's mess,' etc.

2.4 Have you already been reprimanded or chastised for your lackadaisical attitude in this area?

☐ Yes
☐ No

If YES, by whom?

Name		Relationship to you	

2.5 Please give the name of the person most likely to take up the slack when you goof off

Name		Relationship to you	

2.6 How would you describe their current attitude to you?

☐ Very pissed off
☐ Quite pissed off
☐ Fine
☐ Quite happy
☐ Very happy

2.7 If your application is successful, what do you plan to do with the additional time and resources that will become free due to your permitted shirking?

☐ Learn a musical instrument
☐ Flirt with sexy neighbour
☐ Read
☐ Drink
☐ Take drugs
☐ Just chill
☐ Watch TV
☐ Work on my novel
☐ Playstation
☐ Other (please specify)

2.8 If your Shirk Permit is granted, will your chosen neglect affect any of the following areas in your life?

Tick all that apply

☐ Finances
☐ Health
☐ Emotional wellbeing
☐ Social standing
☐ Career
☐ Family life
☐ Sex life
☐ Relationship

2.9 On a scale of 1-10, with 1 being 'not arsed' and 10 being 'bricking it', how concerned are you about this?

☐ 1 ☐ 2 ☐ 3 ☐ 4 ☐ 5 ☐ 6 ☐ 7 ☐ 8 ☐ 9 ☐ 10

2.10 If your Shirk Permit is granted, will your chosen neglect affect any of the following areas in the lives of those closest to you?

☐ Finances
☐ Health
☐ Emotional Wellbeing
☐ Social Standing
☐ Career
☐ Family life
☐ Sex life
☐ Relationship

2.11 On a scale of 1-10, with 1 being 'meh' and 10 being 'aaaaarrrrgh', how concerned are you about this?

☐ 1 ☐ 2 ☐ 3 ☐ 4 ☐ 5 ☐ 6 ☐ 7 ☐ 8 ☐ 9 ☐ 10

2.12 Final checklist – Have you done the following?

	Yeah yeah	**Whatever**	**I did it, OK?!**
Ensured all information is up to date and correct?	☐	☐	☐
Included all supporting documents?	☐	☐	☐
Supplied return postage for your documents?	☐	☐	☐
Made a copy for your files?	☐	☐	☐

I didn't really pay attention when I was filling out the form, but I'm pretty sure I ticked all the boxes and stuff, so just send me the thing when it's done, yeah?

Signature .... **Date** ....

Temporary Visa to Hell

Welcome to Hell! We hope that your stay will be unpleasant and uncomfortable, but before we can let you in to the Underworld, we need to know a little bit more about your visit.

Complete all relevant sections before handing it to the customs demon at border control.

Section 1: Visitor details

1.1 Name

1.2 Date of birth

DD	MM	YYYY

1.3 Is this your first visit to Hell?

☐ Yes
☐ No

1.4 If NO, please give the date of your last visit

DD	MM	YYYY

1.5 How long do you intend to stay in Hell?

☐ days / months / years / epochs

1.6 Please state the primary purpose of your visit

☐ Business – **Go to Section 2**
☐ Pleasure – **Go to Section 3**

Section 2: Business Travellers

2.1 What is the nature of your business?

☐ Estate Agent
☐ Lawyer

2.2 Do you intend to seek an audience with the Dark Lord Himself?

☐ Yes
☐ No

If 'Yes', what specifically do you intend to discuss with Him?

Section 3: Tourists

3.1 Please indicate which of the following sites you intend to visit during your stay.

You must visit at least two to satisfy the conditions of your Tourist Visa. Agents on site will provide you with proof of visit.

☐ The Pit of Eternal Suffering
☐ Brimstone Falls National Park
☐ Lamentation Street
☐ Chasm of the Damned
☐ Sacrificial Petting Zoo
☐ Cerberus Kennels
☐ InfernoWorld™
☐ The Rebellion War Memorial
☐ Styx Marina
☐ Temptation Island

Section 4: Section 4 - Health and Safety

4.1 Have you been immunised against the following conditions?

- ☐ Leprosy
- ☐ Plague
- ☐ Scrofula
- ☐ SARS
- ☐ Avian flu
- ☐ Ebola virus
- ☐ Boils
- ☐ The insanity that comes from looking into the darkness and seeing all of humanity's disgraces staring back at you

If you have not been immunised for any of the above conditions, you must visit the medical station and undergo a series of humiliating and invasive procedures before entering Hell.

Section 5: Customs

5.1 Did you pack your own luggage?

- ☐ Yes
- ☐ No

5.2 If NO, who packed it for you?

- ☐ Friend
- ☐ Family member
- ☐ Stranger
- ☐ Clergyman

5.3 Are you carrying any of the following contraband?

- ☐ Bible / Torah / Koran / other scriptures
- ☐ Crucifixes
- ☐ Holy water
- ☐ Blessed artifacts
- ☐ Cassocks
- ☐ Dog collar
- ☐ Fruits or vegetables

5.4 Please indicate if you are carrying any of the following items

You are free to do so, but please be aware that Hell already has a considerable surplus and you may have to pay an additional levy.

- ☐ Guns
- ☐ Drugs
- ☐ Knives
- ☐ Explosives
- ☐ Fireworks
- ☐ Pornography
- ☐ Small animals
- ☐ Pornography involving small animals
- ☐ Sex toys
- ☐ Whips
- ☐ Chains
- ☐ Solvents
- ☐ Acids
- ☐ Monster energy drinks

I state that the information I have given here is the truth and if it isn't, I understand that my stay here may be permanent.

All hail the great Satan.

Signature .... **Date** ....

www.ingramcontent.com/pod-product-compliance
Ingram Content Group UK Ltd.
Pitfield, Milton Keynes, MK11 3LW, UK
UKHW051207260726
13967UKWH00011B/3153

9 781916 037304